Yujin Koyama

# THE PEARL
## Torment and Ardent Love

esthétiques

*Perle (Tama)*, *Éclosion (Fuka)*, first publication in French, Spanish and Japanese.

Yujin Koyama

# THE PEARL

## Torment and Ardent Love

Cover Illustration: © Yujin Koyama, 2009

Yujin Koyama, *Sacred Night: Pearls from Heaven*, 2009
Oil on canvas, acrylic, tempera, shells and other natural materials, 14 x 18 cm

# Yujin Koyama, writer, painter, physician

Yujin Koyama was born in 1949, in Niigata, Japan. Doctor of medicine, he also devotes himself to writing and painting. Alongside novels and short stories, he paints prolifically, having produced over a thousand drawings and oil paintings.

# Yujin Koyama: A Chronology

1973    Two of his paintings are selected for the exhibition of Shinseisaku[1] while he is still a medical student.

1974    One man show in Tokyo.

1978    One man show in Paris.

1996    Shincho prize laureate for his tale *Mammoth tusk* (original title *Manmmosu no kiba*).

---

1    New Art Society (Shinseisaku). In 1936, seven young Tokyo artists proudly announced the founding of a new art society called Shinseisaku. They declared they would not participate in any official exhibition in order to hold on to their anti-academic positions, and that they would never take part in any exhibition whose philosophy on art was different from theirs in order to preserve their originality. Refer to bilingual site about Shinseisaku

2009    *Incubation*, (original title *Fuka*)

2011    Selected for the exhibition Memorial Aoki Nishinippon[2].

2014    *Pearl*, (original title *Tama*)
        The novels *Incubation* and *The Pearl* were written alongside the
        production of paintings in the simultaneous pursuit of both nar-
        rative and graphic themes.

2014    *Incubation* and *Pearl* are translated from the Japanese into French
        and Spanish.

2015    Monographic video display at the International Museum of Fine
        Art Glass in Abano Terme, Italy as part of a one man show.
        See the website of the Museo internazionale del vetro d'arte e delle Terme,
        on : http://www.museodelvetro.it/

---

2    The Memorial of Aoki Nishinippon Art is part of the Ishibashi
fondation

# The Generous Art of Yujin Koyama

The life and work of Yujin Koyama are marked by a great generosity, though the word should be used sparingly to define the particular action I have in mind. I refer not to the significant though more mundane generosity evident within the limits of personal means, but rather to the openheartedness, the goodness, and the force which we find in those artists who have experienced a pure love for what they do.

Generous actions were ubiquitous in Koyama's early life in Tokyo. Demonstrating acute scientific intelligence at a young age, success in his medical studies led him to a distinguished career in Psychiatry, pioneering numerous important therapies. Yet, despite advancing his chosen scientific field, he was equally well-known for organizing artistic events, and for giving full reign to his own creative vocation, both as a writer and as a visual artist. Indeed, uniting the separate realms of enchanting expressive vision and professional medical practice, to this day Koyama actively incorporates visual art therapy in his approaches to psychology and psychiatry.

Koyama's painting ranges from delicate early pastels to the intense expansive forms and bright colors of his maturity; his writing is similarly possessed of varying but mutually enriching elements – romanticism, fantasy, and allegory combine harmoniously in his narratives. Exquisite floral themes, vibrant seascapes, and animals, such as horses and deer, spectacularly punctuate Koyama's canvases. His influences, whether from nature or mythology, enable us to share a wide-ranging creativity intimately interrelated with a respectful conception of nature. The luminosity, richness and transparency of the colors in Koyama's works, far from being merely figurative elements, open our minds to the pleasures and the force of faerie-like landscapes, and this luminous transparency prompted fellow painter Giampietro Cudin to describe Koyama as 'a warrior of light'.

It is tempting to hastily associate Koyama's pictorial and literary universe with the contemporary vogue for fantasy fiction, and its inevitable and increasingly overfamiliar gallery of magically gifted stereotypes. In fact, Koyama's mythological and fantastical themes are clearly derived from a lifetime's engagement with the spiritual and otherworldly dimensions of Japanese literary and religious culture. For example, the bird in the novel *Incubation* was inspired by the sight of Hokusai's superb painting of a phoenix on the ceiling of one of the principle buildings in the Ganshoin temple in Obuse in the province of Nagano.

And in Koyama's oeuvre we can witness a softening of the conventional oppositions and irreducible binaries of tradition, perhaps most notably in his profound absorption and application of both Oriental and Occidental aesthetics. His vision of perceived phenomena liberates the spirit from the confrontation typically established as dichotomies in art and fiction.

According to Mircea Eliade[3], one of the modern period's most erudite historians of religions, art, in tandem with spiritual awareness, has the power to anticipate crisis and abolish harmful dualities in order to restore primordial unity, and harmonize the polarities which result in catastrophic conflicts, such as war. Whether the antagonists are armies or the individual confronting himself, humanity becomes unbalanced in the perception of major dilemmas or dislocated phenomena. Yet art can heal us when we are in

---

3     Mircea Eliade, *The Sacred and The Profane: The Nature of Religion*, Harcourt Brace Jovanovich, 1987

conditions of disjoint or dissociation, and can encourage the conception of our spirituality as a material, physical form.

Thus, we depend on art as we depend on dreams, for both are remedies of a kind, which assure us of the unity that we fear to lose or that we wish to restore. Koyama is one of those artists whose work transcends the standard polarities, leading us towards an aesthetic appeasement, and liberating us from the inner conflicts born of our disrupted vision. His images strive to relocate man and nature are in the permanent continuity essential for our survival.

As a student trainee in Psychiatry at the end of the 1970's, I can remember the extent to which the concepts of the body and the soul were generally perceived as isolated entities, and how my professional orientations and beliefs were adjusted during my first encounters with Koyama. While Occidental psychiatric thought at that time focused on a body empty of soul or spirit (or whatever other names remain to be invented for our essence), in a series of inspiring conversations, Koyama enlightened me on the progress in biological knowledge of cerebral activity, developments which do not exclude the possibility of the soul. In what might be called at this point a global vision, he stressed the potential in resolving the duality between the material and the immaterial, and reassured me in my intuition of the continuities between the organic and the inorganic, and between the natural world and mankind.

Koyama's unique pursuit of multiple activities can be justly appreciated in the Buddhist philosophical context, where life's timeless absolutes of giving and receiving are perceived as a single unified action[4]. This invitation to the wisdom of selflessness informs Yujin Koyama's artistic vitality.

*Marie Parra Aledo, 2016*

---

4    The Tibetan concept of *'gtong len'* means giving and receiving. See *The Tibetan Book of Living and Dying* by Sogyal Rinpoche, HarperSan-Francisco, revised edition, 2012.

# THE PEARL

## Torment and Ardent Love

# I

## Smiling as I Fell

I really cannot say why I fell.

The sensation of a sudden vacuum inside my ear.

And then, for a split second, a popping sound within my eardrum, as though my ear was collapsing inwards, as though the bones were crushed inside the cochlea, creating a rattling noise, and vaguely reminding me of the anatomy of the inner ear. And then a more explosive crack, and at the same time the sound of a woman's shrill cry, followed by the laughter of light-hearted girls. And then a more triumphant tone, like that of Mozart's soprano Papagena in *The Magic Flute*.

The sounds spread out through the air, over the buildings of the city like squawking birds.

I was terrified, my body petrified like a piece of wood, my limbs seized by rigor mortis. I felt myself being pulled, as if a sticky thread had been glued to me, tracing a line attached to the cochlea, and becoming worse the more the pulling sensation increased.

Falling into this whirlwind, my temple hit a stone, blood spurted, then a tremendous crash, as if all the windows of a building had broken, raining down a hail of glass shards. I could not understand why in broad daylight I was plunged into the darkness of a cellar.

"Ha! Am I inside a seashell?" I cried, imagining myself at the very bottom of the interior of a giant conch shell. There was a powerful, deafening sound, like a long roar, as if someone was blowing into the conch shell. Then the sound of trumpets, ominous, threatening.

Somehow, above all, I had to avoid becoming dispossessed of what I was carrying. A Pearl, which I held closely, and polished constantly. It had not been damaged in the turmoil. I had to keep in mind that the Pearl was a treasure to be protected at all costs, and in my confusion, my worst fear was that it would be stolen. Obviously, someone wanted to take it. Maybe the ear-splitting soprano! Why not? I felt I saw her sharp eyes on me, gloomy shadows floating in mid-air. I felt sure she was approaching in the form of a demon, and I clung to my treasure, which I would have defended to the death, rather than let her have it.

In a mental confusion of nightmarish apparitions I thought that whatever happened I must fight this enemy.

I seemed to be drawing a veil after me, defining a graceful curve, and drifting on the air. Pure white images floated before me.

A feeling of resentment set in, a groaning wave of anger, which made me want to resist. The next moment I was certain of only one thing: I was utterly exhausted. Then the evil presence vanished, I collapsed, and I found myself being sucked, floating slowly down into the depths of a spiral-sided cave.

## II

## How I Conceived the Pearl

With my eyes closed, I saw a cypress, painted in the style of Vincent Van Gogh, swaying gently. At the same time, I felt that my calf was wrapping around on itself, and becoming cold. I hobbled home because of my twisted leg, wondering if I was in my own body. In a moment of acute awareness, I tried to explore what I supposed to be my home, assuring myself that the key I held to unlock my door was not a safety key like those one uses in mental hospitals. I lay down, and touched my bed sheets to be sure that they were mine, and that I was not on a stretcher in an emergency room. I was in my own house near a lake in Musashino. I breathed a sigh of relief and stretched out on my bed, having a throbbing sensation in my temples. I saw myself climbing an endless spiral staircase, shaped like a snail's shell. Its harsh metallic structure corresponded to an artist's desire for originality and imagination.

Being caught up in this scenario did not produce delirium or ecstasy in me, but, by way of contradiction, inevitably returned me to the nightmare.

I must relate that before becoming an artist, I was employed in a company, which cut jobs mercilessly, including my own. Yet, since this painful dismissal, I have experienced a kind of rebirth. Was this not the crux of the issue? I was dismissed when the "bubble burst" and the subsequent Japanese financial crisis took place. There is no need to go into detail regarding my suffering, but suffice to say, my entire body regularly shook, and I sank into a profound depression. At that time, no one could have imagined that I would turn to the arts. But I did. And, as if by magic, I blossomed in my painting. Is it not from this point that the Pearl began to lead me? I paced the city's districts in a stupor, working occasionally in tempera, and using warm colors, such as red coral. I found this, in turn, warmed my heart. In fact, I always had the ambition to become a full-time artist, and always painted, even when I was employed by that soulless company. And now, at last, my dream was most certainly materializing. I did not try to find alternative work, a decision which left me struggling financially, and led to the loss of my family. Rather, I wanted to submit myself to public judgment in exhibitions. Unfortunately, this resulted in my facing further rejection. Nevertheless, the only thing that mattered to me was to preserve the light, this lunar glow that now penetrated my flesh. However small it may have been, I intended to nurture any moon drop, any source of illumination, the slightest ray of light. As the foreign body penetrates the flesh of the oyster to create a Pearl, so in the act of painting, images flowed onto the canvas, and in the same way that the oyster transforms, protects, and shapes the foreign body within it, so I was shaping my Pearl. Immersed in my art, putting my problems aside, combining charming western techniques with the gentleness of *nihonga*, and driven by an energized imagination, I created a world on canvas consisting of fantastic animals and human figures. And finally, customers began to arrive for my work.

My inspiration did not leave me. I entitled a certain work in which I wanted to represent the melancholy reflected in a young woman's face, "Bewitched by a Curse". I held a private exhibition that was immensely successful. All my doubts vanished. It was a hiatus in my war against adversity. Now I was able to hold my head up high in the dark. Indeed, all my paintings sold out on the very day of the preview. It was a triumph. Now I could get back at the mockers, and my previous misfortune ceased to be a subject for their humor. However, my success had not been immediate, or without hardship. I had worked as if crazed. I drank a great deal to keep my energy levels high, but in the end discovered I was losing my physical vitality. A psychiatrist gave a tongue-in-cheek diagnosis of a "disease of creativity", but I knew very well I was neither mad nor sick. My blood boiled. In the heat of creation, the viscera and every muscle of my stomach burned to the depths of my kidneys. I felt pins and needles in my fingertips, which then began to ache for painful minutes at a time. Blood sprang from the bottom of my heart. And at this very moment, I became aware of the Pearl's presence in my flesh. Sirius sparkled in the winter night sky as if the love of a woman had filled my heart. Coldness and any lack of gaiety had gone. I had the feeling that I was protecting the most precious lapis lazuli of ancient Mesopotamia, as if my insides had been themselves the flesh of an oyster concealing a Pearl. I considered it, nestled in the fragrant warmth of my skin, stroking it as if it were a loved one. Newly single, would I be able to find something else higher than this Pearl, that could bring me to a state of euphoria, such as the dream of eternal love to which everyone aspires? Was there somewhere someone who loved as strongly as I loved my art? At every meeting I took part in, I couldn't see such a one. I became a rude and impatient individual. Friends of mine considered my behavior a form of suicide. I confided in an acquaintance, who claimed to be a poet, only to discover that my story was of no interest to him.

Another time, a musician of great sensitivity took my works into consideration. He asked me to collaborate on a project. He would compose music which echoed the rhythms of my paintings. One of my images was projected onto a big screen, with musicians placed below at the front of the stage. It was a fantastic experience, and I remember that when I heard the music, the sound of the marimba, in particular sounded wonderful to my ears. I was moved to the innermost depths of my self, and plunged in delights worthy of Dionysus. Was my talent so great that it could arouse such rapture and pleasure in others? This musical dimension revealed a new brilliance to my Pearl, and now there was an eternal place for it in my heart. Unfortunately, there were not frequent opportunities to feed my desire. Moreover, I was faced with the eternal threat of losing the Pearl, and this grieved me. And then, to my horror, counterfeits of my paintings began to circulate. Furthermore, I had to enter into expense to defend myself against spiteful criticisms, which were nothing more than gossip. Vague acquaintances pretended to be the closest of friends against all expectations. Then, conversely, a trusted friend of mine of many years suddenly went silent about my art, while another, who had become extremely and unexpectedly rich, turned away from me. Success keeps you confined in the gilded prison of honors, where there is nothing to boast about. In truth, my only goal was to protect what mattered most to me, and this remained an unwavering obsession. But how could I avoid the depression that drove me into endless solitude? I loved the Pearl more and more as it grew inside me. The creative energy which flowed continuously from the bottom of my being, let out an infinite number of images onto the canvas, and I knew that if I did not stop listening to the secret whispers of the Pearl, I would never yield to any threat or to any anxiety.

# III

## Fleeting Light and Devilry

I was determined to follow my own way, protect the Pearl as well as possible, and continue to shine and polish this delicate treasure like a faithful craftsman in order to increase its beauty.

First of all, I studied my immediate environment, starting with my studio ceiling. It was a dome resembling a boat's sail filled with the sea wind. In its widening center, I installed a conduit with a faceted light reflector. It made me think of a dragon's tail twisting towards the sky. Light was transported through a metal cylinder, and diffracted in colored beams by means of a finely cut prism.

A glass container - a large round Italian vase - was on the table just below, and was filled with all the colors of the rainbow, offering an enchanting effect. I burned incense of myrrh at night. In the smoke that emanated from the center of my studio, when abundantly flooded with moonlight, there would suddenly appear sparks of golden dust, moving in beautiful waves of light. That is why I later called my device "the marvelous light machine". My body shook and the tears of my soul resonated like marbles scattering on a floor. The little sparks which floated in the rays of incense smoke recalled to me a *haiku* I had read the day before, which, like this evening, featured a night of a full moon.

> *On a clear night in late winter*
> *the moon crosses the sky*
> *bringing a star.*

I laid my treasure on the floor and covered it with blue tiles placed side by side like a wavy mosaic, sparkling with moisture. I planned to add a marine element to the Pearl, although we were in an urban area. My project was to envisage the process that would lead me to the creation of an unquestionable masterpiece. I had in mind the famous work entitled "Metempsychosis", an ink drawing on a silk scroll, which Taikan Yokoyama painted at the end of his life.

I was wrapping the Pearl when an unwelcome visitor arrived. His eyes fixed to the ground, he seemed to want to surprise me at work. Maybe it was the incense fragrance and the troubled atmosphere filled with smoke which added to my confusion. Anyway, I experienced a dizziness, and an intuition of danger. Maybe this passion had the power to summon evil spirits. I felt myself to be a prisoner of a Pearl that harbored an evil spirit, and anxiety oppressed my heart more than ever. A permanent whistling in my ear added to this strangeness and I thought my destiny was sealed. Whatever transpired, I had to escape this tinnitus!

# IV

## Tinnitus

It became vital to consult an ENT specialist in order to solve the distressing problem of tinnitus and drag this devil from out of my ears. It was with no small degree of embarrassment that I visited an otorhinolaryngologist. Using a tuning fork, the physician felt my forehead and my head, and asked me questions about the sound of water I was perceiving in both ears. He wore a medical mask, and as he was increasing the volume of sounds that he made me listen to, he pointed to the intersection between both parts of the inner ear on an image representing the cochlea projected onto the wall. I heard a sharp noise like the sound of two metallic objects crashing together. Vertigo seized me to the point that I thought I would fall out of the chair, while the specialist, without any feeling, went on speaking of hallucinations, staring at the image of the cochlea, and specifying that there was indeed an injury! I did not consider his explanation satisfactory. The doctor asked me how I felt. I stared at the image of my ear. I stood up, weakened and mystified. I knew any hope of successful treatment would be in vain, and it was dreadful for to me to read in the predictable diagnosis just how much this was the case. Holding in his hand a prescription for a diuretic that would, according to him, relieve too high an intracranial pressure, I went home quickly.

I drank the liquid prescribed. It had the bittersweet taste of gin, which warmed my tongue but did not make me drunk. If there really was a problem with the lymph, which would have resulted in edema, I could now expect that soon I would be free of this problem. But over the following days, I heard a thudding noise. Like a groaning coming from within a forest thicket, the tinnitus and the continuous fizzing were, therefore, not going to go away.

I had a nightmare in which I saw myself pushing back the cochlea snail with his perfectly round eyes crawling over my cheeks. I perceived deep in my ears something like the gushing of a geyser, or the splashing of water in a bathroom. Or the beat of flowing blood. Wanting to bang my head against the walls, I escaped from this tormenting whistling by sinking into madness.

## V


## A Visitor


Ten days or so after the "shell delirium" and its strange stories, a young man with a juvenile and anguished face came to see me in my studio. I had begun opening on Sundays to give classes and welcome those who were interested in my paintings. I did not want to hide my work. I wanted my paintings to be the basis for controversial but fruitful meetings in which we would confront our life experiences. Nevertheless, I was more focused than ever on polishing my Pearl.

The young man of around thirty years old was called Ootani Senichi. He was a surgeon at the hospital. From an early age, he had shown artistic aptitude and I was extremely pleased with a visit from a person of such personality, even if it occurred only once.

Short hair, square face, confident, robust. I noticed these traits as well as the damaged skin on his hands, which was certainly due to the disinfectant he used in his trade. He had the thin fingers of the gifted surgeon. Suddenly, I imagined those hands intervening in human organs with indifference, moving through seas of blood. The French word "sangfroid" came to mind, literally translated into Japanese as "to have cold blood", to possess the ability to perform an action calmly. There was an absence of any limit between calmness and cruelty in this strong young man's expression, and I began to feel the internal discord existing within him.

He, not perceiving my thoughts, absently looked around the studio, raising his head toward the ceiling, and keeping his head straight, even though the ground seemed to undulate gently beneath him because of the swirling light emitted by my machine. And, with a detached air, he grimaced, as if he were about to comment that he had entered the strangest of places.

It was by chance that we were both from the same area, a region of abundant snow, and that in high school, we were among the youngest students. Though he was close to me in age, he liked to consider himself the older. Suddenly, he remarked, "I would have killed myself if there were no such thing as art. Without it, I would have gone insane."

At my astonished expression, he, in turn, looked surprised, and then continued, "At the same time, no doubt, art is a double-edged sword, because there are painters who paint and commit suicide as well. The act of painting can also be a poison that leads the mind to madness."

Listening to him, I smiled and nodded. And then suddenly I wondered if it could be that this young man who spoke so abruptly, could have known something about the existence of my Pearl. And then I saw him in a different light. "I would now like experienced and recognized painters to save this work that I will not be able to finish."

And saying this, he pulled out of a cloth bag a painting composed of three canvases, picturing Saint Anthony slaying demons and devils, as he often appears in brilliant masterpieces of the European Middle Ages. It was a representation of the saint holding a gleaming sword. The technique lacked confidence, but the image had a real strength. He must, therefore, have truly battled hard to produce this painting with its half human creatures and apparitions in the form of prehistoric birds and poisonous toads at the feet of the central character, wielding his shining sword against them. Yet what did he wish these figures to mean?

Again, I observed the young man differently. I no longer saw him as I had at the beginning of our encounter. I looked at him more closely and noticed that despite his apparent spiritual strength, his eyelids were twitching slightly, as if he had been frightened by something.

As if offended, he lowered his head and changed the subject by saying, "Anyway, sir, would you like to see the way I paint?"

He put his canvas on one of my easels, holding a flat brush in his right hand, and prepared to paint. The hand and the tip of the brush trembled. Was this what one calls "writer's cramp" or a state of sudden uncertainty? What I saw was very cleverly designed. He was about to put a small amount of paint onto the canvas as best he could, when, after a moment, the brush fell. He looked up to heaven, and like a wounded bull, uttered a low growl. Meanwhile, the left pocket of his shirt swelled. He grabbed and tugged.

Clearly distressed, he took from his pocket a small white box. I was skeptical, absorbed in my thoughts, despite watching him hold the small white plastic box before me.

It contained a so-called white "god's conch" and carried its registration number in blue ink, probably that of the production center, while the label name was written in small print.

I asked myself again why a human being should appear as a shell? Hypersensitive as I was, I always reacted to surprises with emotion, and I could not help suspecting him of hidden motives. I heard a sudden thud as my mind was torn by two oscillating conditions: on the one hand, a great clarity of thought, and on the other, a distracting confusion. Although fully aware of the young man's presence, I began to shake. He put the little box down.

"This shell is fit only to be thrown away, but I could not do so, and so I keep this immaculate whiteness by my chest."

I was worried about how this young man talked, but as he had adopted this white conch (another consciousness disappearing with the body!) how could I be blinded by a form that had never been a spiral shape? A vertiginous feeling announced the beginning of yet another phenomenon, and the terrible noise of a shell in the bottom of my ear made me think that this was an illusion produced only by a smaller shell.

The young man stared at me, giving the impression that I had been struck and was trying to hide. He murmured suggestively, "After all ... for you ... sir ..."

This was profoundly irritating, and I could not help but ask what he meant.

"Actually, I had a similar symptom. The depths of a shell with sticky tentacles appeared to me every night. When I was in agony in this nightmare and I woke up, pajamas in a twisted mess on my body, my stomach churning to the point of vomiting, the apparition rolled up clumsily like a shell. I called this "the delirium of the shell.""

I felt as if I had hugged a woman, and danced crazily, angrily in love and suffering the deep jealousies of an affair.

"I am very surprised to hear that. But I think I understand what you are talking about."

The interest eventually passed. The young man changed his position in my studio, and I smiled coldly. Remaining calm, I asked him, "Are you a man or a prophet?"

In the evening, as I returned to my home, I was haunted by the sensation that the shadow of a spiral shape was following me, wrapping itself around my feet. Had this young surgeon bewitched me with some dark supernatural power? Was he mocking me by means of artful magic with the hallucination of the bright screeching insect that turned around me?

The brilliant half-moon clarity was unlike any I had seen before, but I had never yet exposed the Pearl. Or was this a lie? I found this thought regrettable. But then my ecstasy came back, and I drank a glass of excellent sake, dancing on the traces of the brilliant spiral, which emitted a piercing laugh, like a shout of victory thrown up to the heavens. Then a terrible movement began again, this time in the middle of my stomach and travelling right up to my heart. I stopped breathing, only to witness a noxious insect climbing onto my body, which as before, stiffened and hardened. I had learned that fighting was not to my advantage. It was a night passed in transpiration and self-torture.

# VI

## A Crescendo of Feelings

The next morning, still feeling drowsy, I woke the young man up to discuss what had happened. He was slowly sipping his coffee, his expression confident as if he knew what I was going to say. As I was obviously becoming angry, and on the verge of an explosion, he began to speak:

"I know exactly what you have experienced. At first, I too wondered anxiously if  was suffering hallucinations or was delirious. But with the help of someone to whom I will be forever grateful, I did not succumb to delirium."

"Ah! And ... Who was that?"

"A woman ... that you know ... An artist, who passed away two years ago. We never understood why she died." That surprised me, but he repeated, "A woman ..."

Her name was Rikako. I knew her. She was beautiful and

independent, and had inspired in me strong feelings of both love and rejection. She had drowned two years ago. The body was found in the Dobu River, close to her home. I heard about it a year ago. She had shown signs of weakness and terrible mental distress. Her emaciated face had completely lost its beauty. Her speech was incoherent and she never went out anymore. She had reached her zenith as an artist a little before 1978. A precursor of a new style of narrative painting, she had acquired a large audience. She painted long dark haired women, curved and sensual, with thin lips, and slightly swaying narrow hips, which did nothing to diminish speculation amongst male artists. They wondered if she would pose for them.

Ah, so this young man had also had a relationship with this woman ... This connected us even further.

I had had a more or less formal relationship with her. It was just before my own paintings were beginning to sell. We became intimate quickly. I felt the strength of her regard when she turned to me, like an eagle fixing its prey. The wild soul of this passionate woman with a beautiful face was to make me one of her conquests. Coincidentally situated in close proximity, we divided our time between our respective studios, discovering and revealing to each other the secrets of our art and the paradise of our beings. During this time, the studio of a renowned artist was also a paradisiacal place offering an abundance of exquisite fruits. Her own was a bright treasury, filled with precious jewels.

However, this cruel woman blew hot and cold, alternating between love and hate, disappointing and shattering the delight of my affection for her. Due to the coldness of her heart, she fought against her own talent, and gradually descended into despondency, even though I was with her. Even today I am stunned that she could produce any paintings at all in the condition she was in.

As I have said, I suffered animosity and attacks from my peers, but she was the most aggressive of all towards me. She began to criticize my painting bitterly and with remarkable cynicism, and she never hesitated to insult me, even in public at those meetings where one always finds one of the rising artists of the moment.

"You've imitated a painting of mine which I care very much about," she suddenly cried on one such occasion, continuing angrily, "It is certain that your "Bewitched by a Curse" is a copy of one of mine. And you know better than anyone how important my works are to me. Even though you have that incredulous smile on your face, I know that you have stolen my image in situ. You cannot deny it!"

I reacted to this accusation with an intense anger of my own, but although I denied her reproaches, at the same time something told me that her original and my so-called copy were two distinctly different things. She had shown me some sketches which revealed that she had been abused while very young.

My initial certainty of her misunderstanding and confusion was gradually replaced by an awareness of the reality of my plagiarism, and I regretted it. Yet what if her public denunciation was simply an ambitious plan to keep me close to her, among other things? Why not?

It is true that I have made plenty of imitations in order to reach a very high skill in my own art. But she felt injured because of what she called my pettiness, and which she saw as the predominant trait of my personality. She began to break down, and I  saw her now as disheveled, the beauty of her face having disappeared, and emerging in its place the features of a cold ogress.

"No, do not worry about that," I said to the young man, unnerved by both the severity of our quarrel and the reason that had suddenly driven her to commit social suicide. I noticed that he too still felt compassion for her.

"I had a very difficult relationship with this complicated person."

He burst into tears. Perhaps talking to an older, mature individual was painful for him, and perhaps this had also led him to break down, his confidence destroyed in a whirlwind, just as the spiral that appears as a harbinger is also lost in the chaos that follows. The spiral is shell-like, fully covered, as hard as a stone, and proclaims that feelings will disappear into this vortex that swallows everything. I spoke to him with unfamiliar words. "Your small shell. Why?"

"Feelings are a poison within the poison. Be wary of them as of obsessions."

Saying that, he raised his eyes to heaven. Any disease scares the soul, even that of the young surgeon who plays with it.

## VII


## Stress

The young man's frightened face followed me wherever I went, so that I could not forget it. At home in the evening, opening a door, I stopped, frozen with fear, feeling a strange presence in the dimness of the room. As always, my "marvelous light machine" lit the room beautifully, but that night, it seemed to me that I could sense a floating presence. "What if something has been attracted to the Pearl?" I thought.

My own distorted face was reflected in the light machine, and I felt dizzy. The face seemed to want to scream with fear, but it immediately vanished. Above me floated something like a charm that I recognized. I jumped back, holding my breath, and looking around the room. The shadows of objects illuminated by the light reflected in my machine seemed peaceful as usual. Was what I had perceived a moment before a supernatural presence? Perhaps

I had gained the ability to make visible those imaginary forms I painted, even though I so opposed the tedious representation of phenomenal reality. On the other hand, in the euphoria they brought me, these illusions often seemed to be moments of grace.

Of course, even though one can always say feelings stay "hidden and unanswered", a new conviction was born in me. Someone or something was attracted by the Pearl! The distance between my head and the rest of my body seemed to be gradually diminishing, and I felt a menace at my back. In the morning, I forgot to shave, and while still in my dressing gown I went out to survey the neighborhood. While often turning to consider what was happening, those things that appeared and disappeared behind me made me think that they were related to my painting style, but I could not be completely certain of this. Could it be that this thing that I kept secret, hidden deep within my body, was laughing at me out of jealousy? Think about it. Until then, it was only able to have the company of spirits, of the mountains and rivers. I now needed to adopt a further strategy, and keep my imagination open to all possibilities. This seemed to be the wisest idea, and it excited my rational mind. Whatever my sorrows and my weaknesses were, and even if I was courting disaster, this was not the food and drink that the mind of an artist could refuse. In my opinion, this crisis was due to the charm of the Pearl and to the fear of Hell.

As I went home, treading lightly, I moved away from the bustle of Tokyo and entered a park. There, I was surrounded by rows of cherry trees, and I heard the muffled sound of my footsteps on the grass. The trees in full blossom formed great bunches of brilliant flowers, and I heard metallic sonorities murmuring and rustling in the wind. It seemed to me that another face appeared on the grass in the park, and I felt a chill down my back. I wondered if I had the symptoms of an evening fever, but soon after I was distracted by the tender cherry blossoms as they began to fly about. Then I felt around me a pressure which disturbed my vision, making me see a thin wrinkled skin that peeled off me. As if I had taken off the mask I had been using to isolate myself from the world, my eyes began to widen. Shortly before that, the air that touched my cheeks seemed different.

Then the shadow of someone stopped in front of me. From a distance, a supernatural form approached me. In an extended position on a bench facing the sun, lay a woman. A cherry blossom petal landed on her long black hair. As I approached her, she lifted her head, revealing large eyes under her hair. I thought it might be Rikako ... but, with her bright eyes, I immediately asked myself why it should be her, and why would she be here? Her fascinating smile, which had captivated all men, was inviting me now. "I know something, I who am sought to the end of the earth. The beauty of the Pearl is not lost, as it is equal neither to love nor the spirit world. No!"

With an enigmatic air, she looked at me quizzically, and her fascinating smile intimidated me. I became tongue tied, and without intending to, said, "Ah ... How? No!"

"So. Until the last moment, you will keep up your pretense?"

She gave a scornful laugh, and with a mysterious smile she blinked those eyes, black eyes, as if she were a celestial body from the vast cosmos which held her. An icy wind crept between us. On the grass of the park, swirling around us, as in a storm, countless cherry blossom petals. When all became quiet again, her shape was no longer there. I collapsed on the bench. Only a few silhouettes remained, and the bright reflections of cherry blossoms. I laughed at my mistake. That voice, those black eyes shining ... What a bizarre encounter. What a joke! But then, wherever I was, I felt the pressure of her insatiable tenacity.

Back home, still dazed, whereas until now I had sensed no physical threat, I felt a presence of great weight near my light machine. Would I have the means to defend what people commonly have lost, their passion and dignity, as I felt a gust within me as if my heart was bursting? Surprised by indistinct sounds, I watched intently the side of my chair, my eyes wide open. But there was nothing to indicate any sign of hostility. I was sure that a noise struck my ear, as one should be struck by a feeling. And there is was again! Tinnitus! Like the sound of a flute, rousing me awake. The strange scene of a favorite *haiku* came back to me:

> *Whistling against the hedge*
> *Winter winds tell of the vicissitudes*
> *Of a woman's rich love life.*

It is true that I seemed to hear shrill female voices, but meanwhile, I was horribly afraid of being trapped by some magic trick. Perhaps because of the spell which took hold of me in the cherry blossom park, I was in the presence of Rikako, reincarnated, and maybe I was trying to lean on her shoulder? And perhaps this murmur came from the movement of her black hair? And, perhaps, evil spirits would come up on my deathbed to mock me, provoke me, and drag me to hell?

# VIII

## A Dazzling Dream of Beauty

The disturbing sound coming from the bottom of the shell tortured me, and I could no longer fight against it. Soon after, perplexed, I heard the sound of objects crashing down onto the sidewalks of the city, the streetlights spinning above my head, and the myriads of resounding noises enveloped me.

While I could see this dimly lit spiral staircase, winding into infinity as night fell, I had the feeling of being trapped inside an absurd giant seashell.

"Ah, well. Curtain up! Here then is the beginning of what the young doctor called the shell delirium!" I said to myself, sensing that I was being manipulated - a sensation of enforced paralysis - and I let myself fall onto the couch, staring at the ceiling, and feeling that apart from my knees, my whole lower body was stiffening. Attentive then to the slightest opportunity to leave this trap and climb these endless stairs, something came towards me. A light caused a shadow, which fell over me. And that is when I realized it was a cold light that enfolded me.

I felt the presence of something in a mist, taking the form of a net. A face was approaching, so close that our foreheads almost touched. But, as the apparition wore a halo and was transparent, I was not sure I was alive. However, I was breathing. My anger was unbearable. My face distorted with a feeling of resentment, I curled up in the middle of the painting, my expression childlike. The face, as far as I remember, had a barbed canine under the bridge of the nose. It took my right ear off without sparing a single strand of hair. Where there was a hole in place of the ear, a wet tongue came at the last moment, bursting the eardrum and licking the inside. Nausea, violence and pleasure mingled. This devil's canine did not care about the difference between flesh and blood! Sharp sounds of swallowing came from the bottom of my ear.

My vision darkened. Then, a remarkable snap and something rolling before my eyes. Coming from nowhere, the Pearl appeared. That Pearl that should have been hidden in the deepest part of me, rolling in a pretty dish! More than anything, I wanted to materialize myself in my "marvelous light machine" and even more than this, I wanted this light to illuminate my Pearl forever!

A long finger reached out to the Pearl I was holding. It wanted to magically control me. Grabbing the Pearl, I kept it in my closed hand, though gently.

That intense jealousy can join the feeling of surprise caused by the sight of beauty is not new. My hand gripped the heart of the beauty that this Pearl represented. I felt that I was being triumphantly observed in my agony. A presence full of arrogance, who had the upper hand. I was not going to hide from this face which made me shiver and want to taste the exquisite beauty of the Pearl. Then came the sound of something being swallowed. The sound of swallowing with great delight. I swallowed the Pearl.

Reduced to a deep misery at the sight of this face without expression, staring at me aggressively, in a strange pale light, I saw in the eye's sockets, two Pearls waiting for me! As much as I have loved the Pearl ... Now, I coldly lowered my eyes! Despite the hatred I felt, what else could I do? As might be expected, the Pearl was also bewitched and exceeded the imagination of the artist. From the nostrils in the middle of the face, beads multiplied like smoke sparks. Pearls! Pearls! Pearls! Cascading generously, gliding along a tongue, coming out from the nostrils. One of the Pearls rolled without hesitation out of the nose, coming from the lungs of the white shadow, along the soft tongue. The shadow did a wild, abandoned dance, wearing the Pearls mockingly. I started to climb on the dancing shadow, which was enjoying this dance without paying any attention to me. I had to be careful not to make a mistake. I grabbed the hem of the long floating fabric, white as snow and proudly brandishing my brilliant Pearl, shining with a devilish glow. In the dim light, the spiral staircase continued, unending. I had made that light for the Pearl, and its shadow would rise as moonlight! Deeply moved, I felt different degrees of surprise. I was using bright and juvenile colors and fragrances, as in my painting "Bewitched by a Curse", but Rikako continued to attack and rob me. How could I have trusted this woman? A wonderful apparition of a goddess which, after all, I could never have made possible, even if I had done my best to paint her, now appeared, suddenly, before my eyes.

Along with the soul of the young man, who groped his way along - I noticed his numb hand - the echo of the shrill laugh of the soprano singer reached me. A numb hand, that's all I felt, then nothing.

The light spinning above my head.

*

# By the same author

Translated from the Japanese
  into French and Spanish by M. Parra Aledo
  *PERLE*, 2014
  *PERLA*, 2014
  *ÉCLOSION*, 2013

Translated from the Japanese
  into English by Stanley Anderson
  *INCUBATION*, 2013

Present English edition prepared for publication by
  David John Taylor
  *THE PEARL*, 2016

# Index

International museum of fine art glass, Abano terme, Italy,^9

Nagano, both a prefecture of Japan and its capital city 長野,^12

nihonga 日本画 literally «Japanese-style paintings»,^23

Niigata 新潟,^7

Obuse, 小布施町 located in Nagano prefecture, Japan,^12

Pearl (The), Tama, 珠,^9

Shinseisaku 新制作協会,^8

Taylor, David John, teaches English Language and Literature at the University of Tokyo. His publications include 'Connoisseur of Exile: The Exile as Connoisseur: The Travel Writings of Bruce Chatwin', and 'Shaking the Buddhas: Lafcadio Hearn in Japan,^53

Yokoyama, Taikan 横山大観 (1868–1958),^28

THE PEARL Torment and Ardent Love

Printed in April 2016 by BoD GmbH, Norderstedt, Germany

©© Esthétiques, France, 2016
ISBN 979-10-95769-07-1
Legal deposit: second quarter of 2016